Shapes and Sizes
Table of Contents

Bendon Publishing International, Ashland, OH 44805
© 2004 Disney Enterprises, Inc.
Based on the "Winnie the Pooh" works, by A.A. Milne and E.H. Shepard. All rights reserved.

Name: _____

Circle

  Help Piglet. Trace the **circles** with the correct colors. Then, color them in.

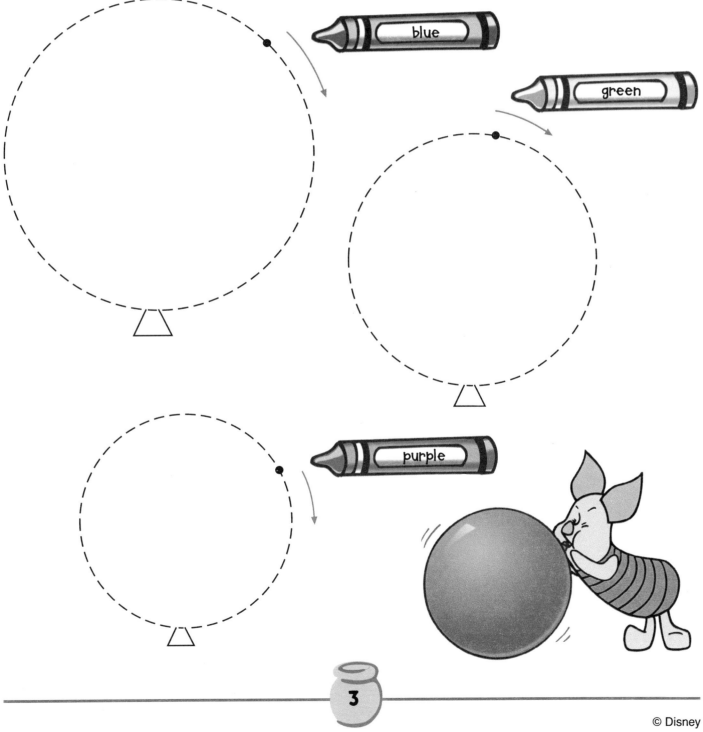

Name: _____

Square

 Complete the drawing by connecting the dots in order from 1 to 5. Look at the front of Tigger's jack-in-the-box. It is a **square**. Color the picture.

Name: _____

Triangle

Look at Piglet's boat. The sails of the boat are **triangles**. Color the picture with the colors that match the numbers: 1   ; 2 ● ; 3 ●.

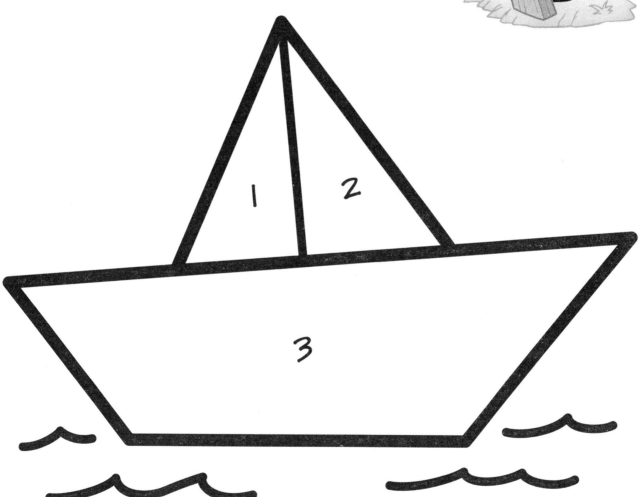

Name: _____

Shape Recognition

Color Roo's puzzle. Color the **circles** red
and the **triangles** yellow. Color the rest
of the puzzle with your favorite colors.

Name: _____

Rectangle

Complete the drawing by connecting the dots in order from 1 to 5. Look at the side of Tigger's wagon. It is a **rectangle**. Finish coloring the picture.

7

Name: _____

Shape Recognition

Look at Piglet waving to Pooh through the window. The window is a **square**. Pooh is keeping his house warm. Pooh's fireplace is also a **rectangle**. There are even two **circles** at the top of Pooh's fireplace. Trace the shapes. Then, finish coloring the picture.

Name: _____

Oval

 Pooh and Piglet want to move the chest onto the rug. The rug is an **oval**. Finish coloring the picture.

Name: _____

Star

 Complete the drawing by connecting the dots in order from 1 to 5. Look at the shape Pooh is holding. It is a **star**. Finish coloring the picture.

© Disney

Name: _____

Shape Recognition

Tigger and Roo are playing together. Trace the shapes. Then, finish coloring the picture.

Name: _____

Shape Recognition

 Christopher Robin loves his new gift. Pooh likes it, too. Trace the shapes. Then, finish coloring the picture.

Name: _____

Matching by Shape

 Help make a machine that will move water for Pooh and his friends. Have an adult help you cut out the shapes on the left. Then, glue each shape in the place that matches it.

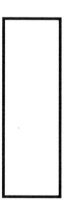

Name: _____

Matching by Shape

Name: _____

Shape Recognition

Look at Piglet's picture below. He used lots of shapes in his drawing. Use the next page to copy Piglet's shapes to make the same picture.

Name: _____

Shape Recognition

Name: _____

Shape Recognition

Look at the cupcake Roo decorated. Then, decorate the other cupcakes to make them all look the same.

Name: _____

Shape Recognition

 Circle the picture that has the same shape as the picture in the box.

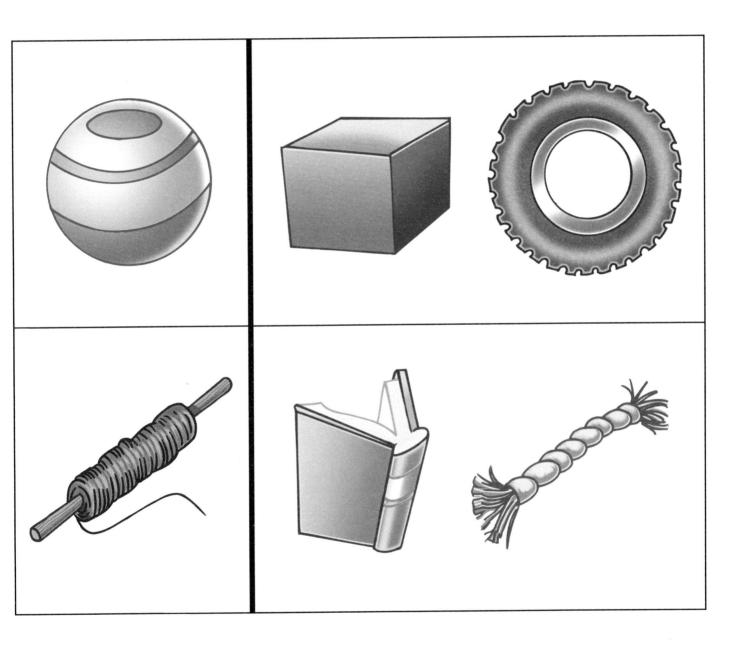

Name: _____

Sorting by Shape

 Look at the pictures below and on the next page. Draw a line from each food to the matching shape.

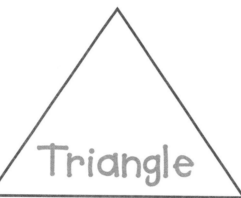
Triangle

Flower Seeds

Rectangle

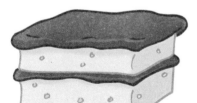

Name: _____

Sorting by Shape

Circle

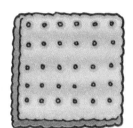

Square

Name: _____

Sorting by Shape

 Help Pooh and Piglet sort their cookies. Have an adult help you cut out the cookies below. Then, glue them on the correct plates below and on the next page.

Circle

© Disney

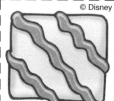
© Disney

© Disney

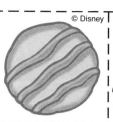
© Disney

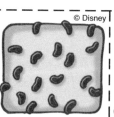
© Disney

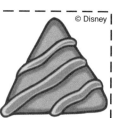
© Disney

22

Name: _____

Sorting by Shape

Square

Triangle

23

Name: _____

Shape Recognition

Help put the pictures back in their frames. Draw a line to match each picture to its frame.

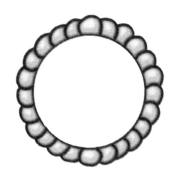

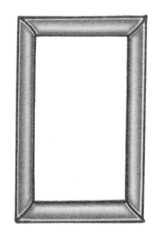

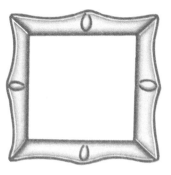

Name: _____

Matching by Size

Draw a line to match each bow to the correct size gift.

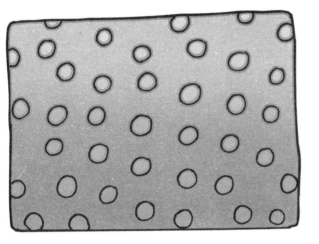

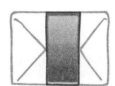

25

Name: _____

Smallest to Largest

 Have an adult help you cut out Pooh's honey pots below. Then, glue the honey pots in order from smallest to largest. Circle the honey pot you think Pooh will choose.

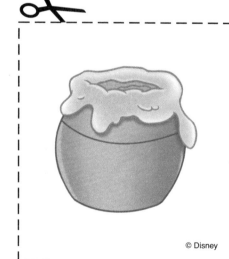

© Disney

© Disney

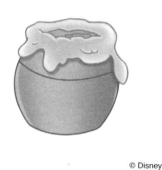

© Disney

26

© Disney

Name: _____

Smallest to Largest

 Number the things by size. Write the number 1 on the smallest thing in each row. Write the number 2 on the next biggest thing. Write the number 3 on the biggest thing.

27

Name: _____

Patterns

 Help Pooh and Roo set out the gifts. Draw the next size gift in the pattern.

Name: _____

Patterns

Help Eeyore and Owl make banners. Draw and color the next shape in each pattern.

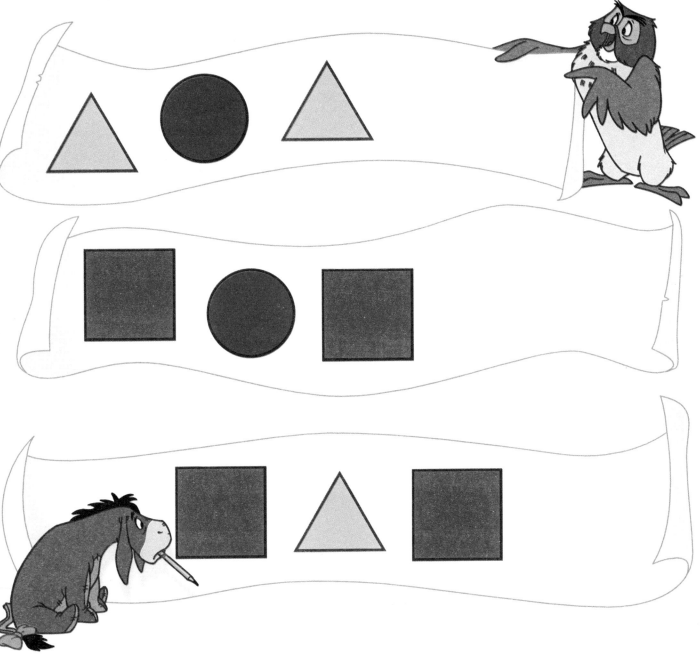

Parent Resource Guide
Helping at Home with Shapes and Sizes

There are many things you can do with your child to practice shapes and sizes. Here are a few activities to get you started:

 Go on a "shape hunt." Encourage your child to look for examples of different shapes around the house. For example, he/she may notice that the clock is a circle and that a book is a square or rectangular shape. Once you've explored different shapes in the house, go outside to discover all the different shapes you can find in your yard and neighborhood.

 Pull out an outfit from your child's baby clothes to compare with his/her current clothing. Not only will you be talking about size, but you will share a fun trip down memory lane.

 Have fun in the water or bathtub. Fill clear plastic glasses with varying levels of water. Have your child arrange the glasses by volume, from least full to most full. You can do the same activity on dry land, just substitute rice for the water.

 Make a "shape book." Staple together several pieces of paper. Draw a different shape on each page. Have your child go through magazines and help him/her cut out pictures of shapes he/she sees. Expand the book as your child starts learning more and more shapes.

 Talk about the word triangle. Link the tri- prefix to other words your child knows, for example, tricycle, tripod, triple, etc. See if your child can figure out what tri- means.

Page 3.

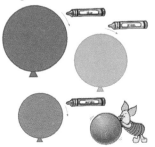

Page 4.

Colors will vary

Page 5.

Page 6.

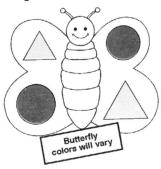

Butterfly colors will vary

Page 7.

Colors will vary

Page 8.

Colors will vary

Page 9.

Colors will vary

Page 11.

Colors will vary

Page 12.

Colors will vary

Page 13.

Colors will vary

Pages 14-15.

31

Page 19.

Page 20.

Page 21.

Page 22.

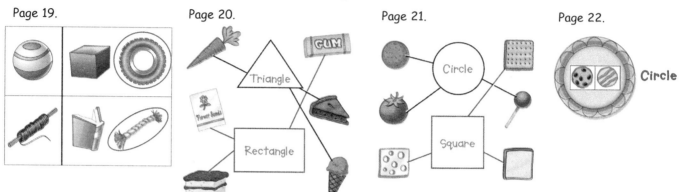

Triangle

Rectangle

Circle

Square

Circle

Page 23.

Page 24.

Page 25.

Page 26.

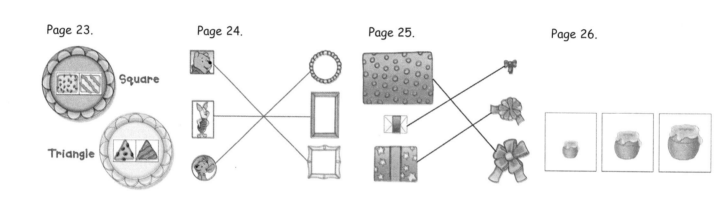

Square

Triangle

Page 27.

Page 28.

Page 29.

1 3 2

3 1 2